Attitude Makes a Difference

by
Fernando L. Soto

Illustrated by
Vladimir Cebu

I0086915

Published by Fate Publishing, LLC.

www.fatepublishsing.com

888-317-8374

FATE
PUBLISHING

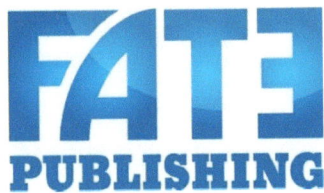

Books may be purchased in quantity and/or special sales by contacting the publisher at 888-317-8374 or support@fatepublishing.com. Copyright © 2016 by Fernando L. Soto. All rights reserved. First Edition, 2016

No part of this book may be reproduced or transmitted in any form or by any means, electronic or mechanical, including photocopying, recording or by any information storage and retrieval system, without written permission from the author and / or publisher, except for the inclusion of brief quotations.

Illustrated By; Vladimir Cebu
Edited By: Rebecca Taylor

This book belongs to:

_____

On a beautiful summer day,
children were running around a school playground
chasing a ball. The sound of laughter filled the playground
until one boy named Norman missed his kick.
"I missed again," he said, "I'll never get this right!"

"You have to think positive,"
said another boy Norman's age named Fernando.
"That's what Miss Smith said."
"But Miss Smith isn't my teacher," answered Norman.
"She isn't my teacher either," said another boy named Charlie.

The children stopped playing and gathered around Fernando.
Even the boys and girls who were in Miss Smith's
class wanted to hear what Fernando had to say.

"How do we think positive?" asked Norman,
"how will that help me play kick ball?"
"Miss Smith said being positive or negative
makes all the difference.
She said if we're negative we can't make things better
but that if we are positive we can."

"Like the little engine that could?" asked Charlie,
"in the end he thought he could and he did."

"That's right," said Fernando,
"Miss Smith read us that book when she was
teaching us about positive attitudes."
"But some things are really hard for me to do,"
answered Norman, "like playing kick ball and tying my shoes.
How can I be positive about that stuff?"

"You can start by thinking that you can do it," said Fernando.
"But what if I think I can do it,
but I still can't do it?" said Norman.
"Yeah, what if?" said Charlie
and a bunch of other six-year olds
that were sitting in the grass listening.

"Then you keep trying until you do succeed," said Fernando.
"You never give up! We need to be positive
for ourselves and for each other.
If we're negative, we have less chance at doing well at stuff."

"I want to try kicking the ball again," said Norman, "but this time with a positive attitude."
"Let's play," said Fernando as he and the others got up and went back to their game.
"Try kicking the ball again," Charlie told Norman.

Norman kicked the ball
that was lying unmoving in the grass to Charlie.
"Yeah, Norman," cheered the six year-olds.
"I did it," said Norman, "but it was standing still."

"The important thing is that you kicked it," said Fernando.
"The more you practice, the better you will get
and one day you will be able to kick a moving ball."
"Because I'm positive," answered Norman.

"You've got it," answered Fernando.
"Miss Smith said a positive attitude will take us
anywhere we want to go, one positive thought at a time.
If you think you can do it you can!"
"Cool," answered Norman.

"Yes, cool," repeated Charlie and some of the other kids.
"Let's keep playing," said Norman,
"so I can practice my kickball and my positive attitude."
"That's right," said Fernando.
"Having a positive attitude makes a difference."

What I learned from this book:

_____

_____

_____

_____

_____

_____

_____

_____

www.ingramcontent.com/pod-product-compliance
Lightning Source LLC
Chambersburg PA
CBHW041241040426
42445CB00004B/114